GOD IS THE PERFECT POET

— Robert Browning

Also by Christopher Vinck

The Voice Of A Confident Woman *(Silver Bow)*
Poems in Celebration of the *Muse* *(Silver Bow)*
Ashes *(HarperCollins)*
Mr. Nicholas *(Paraclete Press)*
Augusta and Trab *(Macmillan)*
Songs of Innocence and Experience *(Viking)*
Only the Heart Knows How to Find Them *(Viking)*
Things that Matter Most *(Paraclete Press)*
The Center Will Hold *(Loyola Press)*
Moments of Grace *(Paulist Press)*
Finding Heaven *(Loyola Press)*
Compelled to Write to You *(The Upper Room)*
Nouwen Then: Personal Reflections of Henri Nouwen
                                 (HarperCollins-Zondervan)
Love's Harvest *(Crossroad Books)*
The Book of Moonlight *(HarperCollins-Zondervan)*
Threads of Paradise. New York *(HarperCollins-Zondervan)*
Simple Wonders *(HarperCollins-Zondervan)*
Threads of Paradise *(HarperCollins-Zondervan)*
The Power of the Powerless *(Hodder) (Doubleday)*
            (HarperCollins) (Crossroad Books)}

RUMORS

ABOUT GOD

by

Christopher de Vinck

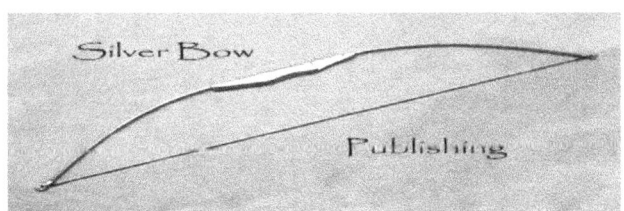

720 – 6th Street, Box # 5
New Westminster, BC
V3C 3C5   CANADA

Title: Rumors About God
Author: Christopher de Vinck
Cover Art, woodcut from the 18th Century: as cited in The Public Domain *Review*
Layout/Design: Candice James
ISBN: 978177403 337-1 (print)
ISBN: 978177403 338-8 (ebbook)
© 2024 Silver Bow Publishing

All rights reserved including the right to reproduce or translate this book or any portions thereof, in any form except for the use of short passages for review purposes, no part of this book may be reproduced, in part or in whole, or transmitted in any form or by any means, electronically or mechanically, including photocopying, recording, or any information or storage retrieval system without prior permission in writing from the publisher or a license from the Canadian Copyright Collective Agency (Access Copyright).

ISBN: 978177403 337-1 (print)
ISBN: 978177403 338-8 (ebbook)
© 2024 Silver Bow Publishing

Library and Archives Canada Cataloguing in Publication

Title: Rumors about God / by Christopher de Vinck.
Names: De Vinck, Christopher, 1951- author
Identifiers: Canadiana (print) 20240529839 | Canadiana (ebook) 20240529847 | ISBN 9781774033371
   (softcover) | ISBN 9781774033388 (Kindle)
Subjects: LCGFT: Religious poetry.
Classification: LCC PS3554.E1165 R86 2024 | DDC 811/.6—dc23

To Roe

Rumors About God

CONTENTS

PART ONE
I heard God plays a violin

I Heard Rumors / 13
I am God / 14
Teaching Elephants How to Dance / 15
Collaboration / 16
Attribution / 17
Evidence / 18
Crèche / 19
Sunday Afternoon / 20
Is It the Voice of God? / 21

PART TWO
There is silence in the snow

Snow is Not the Parable / 25
Evidence of a Second Earth / 26
God in Disguise / 27
God is Everywhere / 29
God or Man / 30
God Intrudes / 32
God's Promise / 33
Life's But a Walking Shadow / 34
Magnificat / 40

PART THREE
When primitive sounds regain meaning

God's Invitation / 43
Perhaps God Resides Inside the Amber Shell / 45
Salvation Hidden in the Rose / 47
Dissertation / 48
Sabbath Morning / 51
Spiritus Mundi / 52
Gratitude / 53
Beatitudes / 54

PART FOUR
Gather round and brush the dirt from your bones

A Gathering at the Cemetery / 57
A Holy Place / 58
God of Light / 59
Argument with the Soul / 62
The Skeptic / 64
Hope under the Autumn Stars / 66
Are You There God? / 67
Genesis / 68
If God Hadn't Created You / 72

PART FIVE
I am told morning is a blessing

Dawn's Blessing / 75
It is a Privilege to Pray / 76
Lord Have Mercy / 77
The Secret of the Sea / 78
God First / 80
Noel! Noel! Noel! / 81
Not Moon, Not Earth, but Heaven / 82
On what Condition Immortality? / 83
Requiem / 84

PART SIX
I know the sounds in the cemetery

Words of an Atheist / 89
What the Shepherds Know / 90
A Boy Named Thomas / 92
Be Attentive / 93
What is Sacred / 95
The Sun is Not a Coincidence / 96
I Think this is What God Means / 97
God of Sunlight / 98

PART SEVEN
In heaven's left side, the green and moss

This Side of Paradise / 103
Hymn / 105
Deep Inside the Winter Lake / 106
Marriage Proposal / 107
The New Testament / 108
Report to the Skeptics / 110
A Blessing / 111
The Secret / 113
Compline / 114
The Farmer's Apology to God / 115

PART EIGHT
I've been to some distance beyond the curl of the sea

The Holy Man Speaks to His Wife Who Just Died / 119
Uncontrolled Laughter Among the Blessed Gods / 121
God of the Forest / 122
Eve / 123
Faith / 128
God Loves You / 129
Genesis / 130
Autumn Prayer / 131
Brush the Dirt from Your Open Bones / 132
The New Astronomy / 134

Rumors About God

PART ONE

I heard God plays a violin

I HEARD RUMORS

Jesus said to him, "I am the way, and the truth, and the life."
—John 14:6

I heard God plays a violin
Made of pearls and strings of ivy.
Each time he plays, flowers drop from his lips
And kiss the earth and the music laughs.

I heard God is easy to spot in a crowd.
He's the one smiling dreams.
I heard if you wake up before sunrise,
You might see God's shadow
Rolling up a bed of hills and spreading
A quilt of lavender.

I was told, in a whisper, God likes poetry,
So I use a basket and place my poems
On pages of straw to comfort the hungry mind.

I heard God holds the earth in his hands
And soothes the edges when the eye of the universe
Becomes irritated.

I heard He likes to ride dolphins.
But does not like to be called Poseidon.
He prefers the name God the Creator.

Visit the philharmonic and pay close attention
To the violinist playing Mozart with his eyes shut.

I AM GOD

"Who do people say that I am?"
—Mark 8: 28

I am God. I am the voice.
I am inside the curl of each sea tide.
When you touch the dew, my tears.
When you feel the sun on your skin, my caress.
When you hold a child
You hold the meaning of my love.

The taste of an orange is from my garden.
When you are afraid at night, I am the moonlight.

If you doubt the air inside your lungs is my whisper,
If you doubt the existence of my shadow,
It matters not ... for I am everlasting..
I am the moisture of the water you drink
When you thirst for me.

When you close your eyes
You are not alone. Even stones are not alone.
Watch how fields of wheat pray together in autumn.

I am the blessing on your forehead.
I am the marrow in your bones.
I walk beside you. I am with you always.
Tell me your story. I will listen.
Sit with me and share what you have lost
And I shall help you find it. I am God

TEACHING ELEPHANTS HOW TO DANCE

***Now faith is the assurance of things hoped for,
the conviction of things not seen. -
—Hebrews 11:1-6***

Is there an ocean in the dry pod?
Is there a whale in the goldfish pond?
I once felt God in a blossom

I sometimes think a shadow is God,
But then the tree curtsies.

Doubt is an empty sail.

I heard God lives at the circus.
Some say he is the ringmaster,
Others say he tames lions.

I heard God is teaching elephants to dance.

COLLABORATION

May God be the glove that moves your hand. –
—Anonymous

How often do you hear "Doing God's work"?

Have you lifted the tide over the beach lately?
When was the last time you balanced
The moon between the earth and sun?
Did you ever create the filigree of a fern,
Or paint the backs of tigers?

The labor of God knows no rest:

Lava needs to be boiled; the edge of lightning
Needs to be sharpened during each storm.
Soil needs rain, air needs to be washed daily
Through the breath of leaves.

God's work?
Making sure fire is hot
And water wet.

Let God be your partner as you work.
Do not despair. Show God your calluses,
And he will show you how to make a world.

ATTRIBUTION

***There is a truth hidden inside
the taste of a raspberry. –***
—Anonymous

God is always at the tip of my pen.
The ink of the Mississippi
Fills the country side of me.
The air of New York tempts me.

I hear God playing a trumpet
In New Orleans.
I see a poem flourishing
Inside my inkwell.

Emily Dickinson wrote
About the slant of light.
God writes in a cursive style,
Not with block letters.

Did you know a pen
Can be a key to heaven?
Did you know a poet
Draws a line from his desk
To the raspberries that laugh
At the edge of the garden?

So what if poetry
Is a collaboration with God.
So what if I plagiarize the horizon
And steal beans from God's garden.
God doesn't need an attribution.
.

EVIDENCE

With God all things are possible.
—Matthew 19:26.

Without God,
The wings of a Dragonfly
Would not be transparent.

CRÈCHE

***Let us now go to Bethlehem
and see this thing that has come to pass,
which the Lord has made known to us.***
—Luke 2:15

The hushed tone of December wind,
Snow perhaps or the neighbor's sleigh:
The bells and reins a single refrain.
With Christmas pulled on the camel's back
Like a traveling cloud in memory,
Let the day and year joyously blend
As we return again to Bethlehem.

SUNDAY AFTERNOON

***And he said unto them,
The sabbath was made for man,
and not man for the sabbath:
—Mark 2:27***

I am alone in this room
During the time of the dolphins,
And the time of the cougars and eagles.
I am here in this room writing.
No one sees what I write
Except the shadows of light against my hands
As I manage this pen and ink.

The fuel of the writer
Is the rain and heat from God
Placed deep inside
The physical self
And translated into a mandate: "Write. Write,"
The alluring whisper to write
As the swan is told to spread its wings
At the park on a Sunday afternoon.

Solitude is my audience,
Words sit beside me in conversation,
Like the fiddle in Tennessee,
Playing a combination of sounds and memory
Condensed in sweet sorrow and celebration.

These walls do not speak or praise what I do.
It is in the breath I take when words or images
Greet me with their assurances
The poem is nearly complete,
And then the silence becomes a symphony
Kissing this Sunday afternoon alive.

IS IT THE VOICE OF GOD?

"Enough to make the spirit moan." — Robert Frost

What is the voice that makes the north wind moan?
It is not the space between the marsh reeds,
Or the howl of a distant wolf
That does not know my name.
It is familiar, an ancient sound emanating
From the cradle of Sunday morning's sighs,
Slightly muffled behind a barrier of wisteria vines.

There is a distance between the image and the sound
Between what is seen and what is hidden,
A no man's land without definition.
A place where pause and insecurity meet
To discuss, in sign language, the meaning
Of what was forgotten and left behind.
And what lies ahead in rows of waiting days?

I do not sense the world with seducing sounds
But more with a collection of oral hieroglyphs
And symbols of cranes and hawks and gulls,
And the liquid figure of a woman approaching.

Who are you, invisible, light but heavy
In the breath of air that surrounds me?
What revered name, what new language,
and what revelation do you bring?

What form do you deign to take:
An ornament like the human body?
A steady stone? A sparkling jewel?
The ego of the oak tree?
The petals of a blue rose?

I hear the moan of a moon-felt cry,
not owl, not bat, not wind
Perhaps my father, perhaps even God.

PART TWO

There is a silence in the snow

SNOW IS NOT THE PARABLE

God asks Job if he has found the treasures of the snow
—Job 38:22

There is a silence in the snow,
Conjured from robes of white
As God unfurls his winter coat
And claims a better heat
Will rise In April.

The earth is cold under the great expanse
Of stiff trees and bare limbs extended.

The wind does not permit a word
With her icy breath
As she surveys the landscape
As if all is calm in death.

I unfurl my arms
And wave my hand
As if I too am God
And sing with full intent
About the future ferns and flowers.
And claim with resolution,

"Snow is not the parable!"

EVIDENCE OF A SECOND EARTH

Be glad, people of Zion, rejoice in the Lord your God,
for He has given you the autumn rains because he is faithful.
He sends you abundant showers, both autumn and spring rains, as before
— Joel 2:23

The new frontier, scraps of bone and memory,
Turns within ourselves in the recognition
That we are ordained to a reverence,
Elongated from past to present,
Stretched along the sea coast
North to south in the discovery
Of the abstraction: eternity, yesterday's soup,
The coming of the next snow or abundance.

Soul and body do notbelong to the old prelates,
Are not born up from glass or concrete
That pretends to dictate violent space,
That ticks like a Swiss clock around the sun.

Each man knows in his heart that he will break,
And such breaking is separate from the machine,
From the wheels and bits of electric impulses
Captured to imitate God or a Holy day.

We are held together with clouds and lions
and bare forsythia in sudden bloom.
We claim a single sound evolving from blue light
And elephants in a circus pacing round and round
In a ritual of some obscure and yet undiscovered eternity.

We are from a second earth,
A candor of desire and cycles brushing against
The wood-dove and snowbird nesting together
In some unfamiliar yet familiar autumn.

GOD IN DISGUISE

Beloved, we are God's children now and what we will be
has not yet appeared; but we know when he appears
we shall be like him, because we shall see him as he is.
--- 1 John 3:2

I see what I see as a blind man sees
With the eyes of the living speaking
As a king might speak, or as the sleepy woman
In her bathrobe bending over to pick up
The morning paper as she notices the dew.

See the jewels I have created: the opal moon,
The amethyst of the sea, the amber necklace
Of dusk preparing for the night.

I speak to the tailor in whispers as she
Cradles the worn grey suit limp in her arms.
I am the mirage across the lake, the flame of a bonfire.
I am the maple in autumn ablaze in reds and yellows.

Listen to the field crickets in summer heat,
Listen to the distinct dog barking in the neighborhood,
Listen to the child breathing in her crib.
I am the voice, I am the hidden music,
I am the symphony as I sit beside the man with the cello
And guide his arms and hands to mimic my voice.

Place a bit of fresh mint on your tongue.
Remember the taste of the orange, salmon, and butter squash.
I prepared these things, my harvest from
The kitchen garden and from the sea.

Close your eyes and recall the texture of sand,
A caress on your cheek, the feel of rain
On your outstretched hand.
I am the hidden way. I am the light
Disguised as the sun. I wear the mask
Not to deceive you but to stand beside you
So you are free to pick a sprig of forsythia

And walk in the new April air
And as you wave the yellow flowers back and forth
To the sky, feel the softness there in the wind.
Feel the glow of renewal and know it is I,
Always the hidden king and pauper beside you.

GOD IS EVERYWHERE

I am a God who is everywhere and not in one place only. No one can hide where I cannot see them. Do you not know that I am everywhere in heaven and on earth?
—Jeremiah 23:23-24

Is God in the stones or in the air that I breathe?
What makes you think God fits inside a honeycomb,
Or even in the color of honey?
Some people believe God arranges the snow
Like laundry on the grass and schedules the rain
At intervals to his liking.

I can understand if God chooses to
Conduct a symphony of Bach, or adjust the wind,
Or distribute the rain and hail and snow
In intricate patterns and soothing melodies.

I read that God walks on water.
Where? In the streams of heaven?
I'd like to lie on a warm summer beach
And see God walking on the water
Feeding the gulls and talking to the fish.

They say God is everywhere
Invisible in his perfect silence,
and visible in his tender touch.

GOD OR MAN

So God created man in his own image, in the image of God he created him; male and female he created them.
— Genesis 1:27

No god knows the meaning of the hieroglyphs in a soul.
No god strokes the first bit of ash upon the forehead,
Makes fire in the shape of a woman. No god knows
The human impulse that defines the hour.

I am my own god, a pantomime of spirit and straw
Held by a stick in the open field under the rain,
Supposed to chase the crows but no more.
I am a monolith of blood and lust so defined.
I use my hands to form the shape of what is to come
And what is to be a sudden loss and win combined.

All women could be defined as fruit and flesh,
An ocean of sweet juice to be poured from breakfast tables
Into our mouths, to swallow, to drink the future and past
In a single stream of milk and passion.

I bath in the sea, not the gods. I pick up the bits of clay.
I scrap shards from my rib. I use oil, marble, perhaps the pen
And words to draw the first lines of you, a universal shape,
More than a landscape, seascape or skyscape.
More than sleek lines of a ship.
More than contours of a beach.

I am the first god, I am the maker of Eve and shadows
With charcoal on canvas, with the words "peach"; "Chalice"
The movement of your hand or the color of your hair.

Do not deny I am the puppeteer,
Giving you life, giving you a name
And the color of your eyes made of glass, made of eggs
And the movement of the sperm whale
Passing through the gray water that spills against your legs.

I'd like to laugh at the gods' creativity,

Their mixed sense of self and fame,
The way they prance and preen
And forget that they do not gamble on the dirt of dreams
And the slick desires of an alley cat.

I am the god, I am the child
Petting the sleek creature beside me.
I am the boy-man, Brahmin, Inca, hawk,
I open my wings, drop my vestments from my body,
I cover my chest and arms with silt and claim elegance
In my greeting you at the lip of the sea,
Expecting you to surrender and willingly comply
With the movement of my words or the chisel in my hand
That has so conjured you from sultry August heat
To winter's clean smoke rising from the Vermont chimney
Or up from a forgotten field of frost
Or steam from the morning dew.

GOD INTRUDES

***Therefore say to the children of Israel: "I am the LORD; I will bring you out from under the burdens of the Egyptians, I will rescue you from their bondage, and I will redeem you with an outstretched arm and with great judgments. I will take you as my people, and I will be your God.* — Exodus 6:6-8**

Are you there God of the iris, God of sea foam?
Did you spit into each shell to make a pearl?
Did you lick the petals; attach them to the stem to build a flower?
Was it your thunder that woke me, a sudden prick of memory? Perhaps it was a summons echoed in the summer night
Carried from note to note on the beating wings of the cicadas.

At first I thought to close my eyes and return to sleep,
Accept your intrusion as an ache in my arm
Or a dream converted to the dark walls and curtains,
But you, spirit, you retained your image,
A man perhaps or a woman with a shroud and veil
I could not see between my waking and sleeping.

Why do you hand me the iris and not the rose?
Do you come from the eye of heaven
Laden with pollen to spread on my lips and forehead?
What do I carry within the midnight of myself?
Roots and seeds, a waiting grave to hold less self
And more the coming blossom of a new breath?

I heard a voice in a language I recognized
Speaking of spring and children rolling hoops
And riding the branch of a maple tree.
Was that you, God? Were you reminding me of the past?
Mimicking the day before, or conjuring what is to come
In a hazily veiled and coded message?
I believe in little gods leaving hints of their existence
Between our waking and sleeping:
An unexpected flower in the yard, a ribbed shell in the sand.
Kyrie eleison. Kyrie eleison. Kyrie eleison.

GOD'S PROMISE

And remember, I am with you always, to the end of the age.
---Matthew 28:20

Find a river, or a secret stream
A place where nothing counts
But the sound of water and
The aroma of moss and air.

Seek beyond the brambles,
Push deeper through the woods
In a downward movement
Though you may think you are lost.

Do not be discourage with crumbling stone
Or a less focused dream.
It is not the path that gives you courage
But the tremble in the voice
And the vision that survives.

When you arrive at the bank's greenery
And wild daffodils
Know this is what I meant
When I promised a lasting life
And reverie of purpose felt
In the silver tear you may weep
In this discovered victory
Of my love and encouragement.

LIFE'S BUT A WALKING SHADOW

Again Jesus spoke to them, saying, "I am the light of the world. Whoever follows me will not walk in darkness, but will have the light of life."-
—John 8:12

I

Tomorrow the heat will arrive from the south
On the camel's back with myths
Of sheiks and gold or the promise of spring.
Tomorrow the creek will break from ice and winter's hold.
The notes of sparrows and the melody of the new pines
Will once again tune themselves to the North wind
In concert with the spinning earth.

For now the closing of the hour, the barn doors shut
Between the house and the end of the day,
With broken bits of frozen earth and the yard is flat.
Look to the distant field, the stage for the coming wheat.
Look to the changing light from dusk to foolish night.
Foolish for those who deny the night holds wisdom
In the interpretation of dreams and patterns in the stars,
If stars are worthy of interpretations.

When there is no moon, the question of self exists
Hunched over the fire that eventually withers to ash.
Light is built from one beam to the next,
From one degree of heat to the next, born out of mist,
Set to illuminate the essential night of drink and laughter.

On what stage, during what sequence do we live?
How do we ask the right questions built on the embers of memory? See
the northern lights, how they appear and disappear
Like gypsies in their gilded wagons and silver earrings.
The sun spits out a blossom of energy and the night
Is illuminated, speared with silver, gold and a blue light.
What is the labor between the sun and earth?
The scythe and the mare's harness hang in the barn;
The scythe, without the wheat, is a bent blade of iron.

The mare with no harness belongs to the meadow, not the man. Begin
with the question: why the sun and earth?
Why the night and flames of the aurora borealis?
Why the number two and why the letters of the alphabet
And why the existence of a single farm in the blue light of April?

The moon might be a god with rooms for girls to dance
Under the chandeliers lit with candles and ether.
Turn aside the tables; make room, the night rises.
Let virtue melt like wax and drip down the sides of their bodies
Coating them with a new polish without shame,
With a new recognition they are built to combine
The impermanent skin and bones with the spirit of self
And the other self in the house of the table gods, and the chair gods.
See how the blue light bends to the yellow light?
Little is omitted from the exchange of light
Between shallow currents and sorrow passing.
The constellations are hidden with such light
After the closing of the day.

II

The house does not fit the landscape, land of ash and pumice,
Land where the trilobites are imbedded inside clay stones,
Land of open graves where spirits rose and receded.
Not in the earth but in the vast deep in another dimension.
Certainly dark, at first, then moist like the open earth,
But something more, a requiem and the movement
Like a violent spring rain and sun combined to force
The new season of the body into the sea-born soul.
There is a possibility for reconciliation
Between the past and future self,
Here in thls grudge of night between the edge of darkness
And the pulsating rim of light,
A summons to choose the coming of the morning dew or
Some other arrival: a dawning, a fashion, a nobility,
Venus hidden in the midnight clouds.
They say the world sits on the back of the turtle
And the turtle goes all the way down to bedrock
And we move with the turtle in slow motion.
Science mocks the turtle and the poem,

And the gods reject what is single: Earth without the sun,
A seamark without the undulating sea, treason without music,
Love without the other born to love.

If you release yourself from the past sorrows and debts,
Images fade and voices echo less and less,
A new distortion quickly replaces what was true
and becomes fading hues and false appetites.

Either the present always existed or it began
As a first explosion of consciousness and light.

Who among us has been born of straw and an idea?
Who among us has not entered the scene from stage right
In sheaths of membrane and blood?
What is the mechanism, birth to birth, death to death,
The rotation of the earth, earth of molten rocks,
earth without an atmosphere?

Now is the prologue of our present selves
Foreshadowing the good air and light.
What breathes fire into the dry wood?
What combination of heat and light defines the remedies
That cure the illness that seeps out of the empty spaces?
What parts of heaven and earth are reserved
For the moment's revelation?
Not clouds or stars of heaven or the wings of angels
Or myths of gates and the music of lyres,
But heaven locked in the stone of the body,
Floating in the slowing blood and brittle bones
Of what precipitates inevitable, eventual death
Of what is to come in the final readiness:
This the anxiety. This the possible flight of dreams.
To wake, to laugh, to languish.
To speak in tongues of fading tales
Sent like larks across the meadow of timeless time
In celebration of the coming spring.

III

Here on the land of fury and haste,
Built under the racing clouds and on molten rocks.
Clouds of desire fade to mist.
Burning dreams cool to solid shapes
And sweat on our foreheads and the shadows of our lost selves Project
against the walls of the first cave.

Do we see what we see or just the shadows?
Do we know what is approaching? What is to come?
Or what the shadows portend in their distorted movements?
I am told we must walk away from the scythe and the horse,
Put away childish things the same way we did so
When we were once children with blocks and tin soldiers.

Niagara Falls is not a god.
The Grand Canyon is not a god.
God is not gold.
Skulls of the coyotes on desert floors
Are not little gods or totems.

How easy to create a desire
To collect coins or paintings of Picasso,
Or to force open the oyster with a sharp sword.
Madness spills into the body not the soul,
The finger reacts to the prick of the thorn,
The scourge of the body detached
From the light begotten from light
Is love of darkness fed with a false light,
Not candle-made but self illuminated.

In solitude happiness is spun from trends of the spirit
Unwinding, unspooling from the body.

Blessed are the pure of heart,
Blessed are those who inherit sorrow.
Blessed are those who walk the primrose path.
Blessed are those who rise above the currents,
And blessed are the cello players.

Here the fury and haste to cleanse the day with spring rain
Is to wash away the soiled snow and yesterday

Into the open flesh of the forgiving earth:
Female, porous, able to absorb the closing of a season.

IV

We do not know what comes between the sea and broken rocks.
We do not know the purpose of the crow in the morning light.
Leaves do not break away from the trees in an arbitrary season.
I can look out to the field in the dying of the light and imagine
Men in feathers and moccasins rattling gourds filled with seeds
Singing to the corn god, singing to the sun.

I look out and see the Neanderthal man, the Peking man,
My father burning leaves n the driveway, smoke surrounding him
Like a mist encircling a dancer in a Chinese robe.

We are pulled between the barn and the house,
The open field and the grave.
What exists between winter and spring that is not discussed?
A hidden season with its own temperature and predictions?
A time where there is no time but a backward glance?
A reverse? A mirror god, a man who becomes a child?
A confusion or lost direction?

Science tells us there is always a partner, always the number two
In the creation of what can be created, in the theory of evolution.
Man does not hate man alone. Man does not love alone.
To dance in hate is to laugh at the trombone;
To dance in love Is to marry the symphony.

V

Do not let the beggars die and the prince give up his throne,
Illness plagues both the weakness and strength of what we know.
To be the combination of saint and fool,
We have the human need for love and solitude.
To be summoned is to be identified as next in faith,
To be divided from mortal company
And join the population of the dead,
The crowd complete with what they brought from the orchard:
Fruit of the vine, evidence of the sun's power,

Stories about the changing seasons
And how they affected the harvest.

We do not cure the body with leeches and the surgeon's knife.

Our fate cries out not for cures or medicine
But for a taste of the succulent orange
And the lips that kiss in both farewell and greeting.

MAGNIFICAT

Oh, how my soul praises the Lord. How my spirit rejoices in God my Savior! For he took notice of his lowly servant girl, and from now on all generations will call me blessed.
--- Luke 1:46-55

Blessed are we who recognize God within us
That we may sing to the lord our salvation
For he recognizes the faults of his servants.

From today to the next day
We shall all be blessed in such realization
For God is not judge but father and forgiveness.
Holy is his name: Allah, Buddha, Abraham, Christ.
Accept his mercy and be merciful
From one embrace to the next.

He has purged pride from the proud
Infused imagined dignity into their hearts.
He stripped kings from their robes
And dressed the poor with his embrace.
He offered the hungry bread of hope
And the selfish the choice of stones or generosity.

May the servants of Israel speak in their books
The stories of his mercy as he spoke to
The fathers and mothers still within us, still,
Within the seeds for the coming spring.

PART THREE

When primitive sounds regain meaning

GOD'S INVITATION

Come, all you who are thirsty, come to the waters.
— Isaiah 55:1

When primitive sounds regain meaning,
Echoes in the chambers of memory
Hidden for a time in my middle sleep,
When sunlight stirs India and China,
Darkness mutes the voice that haunts me.

Silence shares nothing: violin in a black case,
The stillness of bamboo chimes,
An owl that seems to be in a trance or dead
In the grass where I walk.

Is what I hear the clock on the wall,
A rhythm that I do not recognize,
Children speaking French, the bang of a
Ball against the side of the house,
The shrill of the cicadas?

Walking alone aching for company or love
Do I imitate the sound of a menacing crow,
Shout in grief, grab the morning sun
And fling it to the ground and stomp on its light?

There is a voice that repeats itself within me.
Not a wounded spirit or a bear or tiger.
Not the sound of regret or Paris or Bombay.
Not poetry or Bach or the spring warbler.

I am possessed, a ringing in the ear,
A laughter mixed with a guttural plea,
"Be with me. Be with me.
Open my leather case, take out my bow
And play mist upon my strings,
Listen to the north wind and how it sings."
The owl is alive, her wings extended;
She is revived and I fling her into the noon sky
And she cries out "Join me. Join me."

If I had the courage of wings
And the grip of talons to catch the voice
I'd hold it still, clutched in my arms
As soft as feathers and I would listen
To its heartbeat alive ... alive.

PERHAPS GOD RESIDES INSIDE THE AMBER SHELL

***There is the sea, vast and spacious, teeming with creatures
beyond number — living things both large and small.
— Psalms 104-25***

Were you inside the chambers of the shell,
Inside a distant expectation of some well-spring
Where love is found; where I could not define
The nature of self and sorrow?

Were you mingled within
the invisible space deep within
The hidden conditions
I call life or memory?

I could not identify the purity of December,
A month to remember the forgotten names
Of some ritual in the burning of the fir trees.

Little was there in the smoke and ash,
Little to consider in the coming of the New Year
Placed with no conditions except to pass
Once again under the curved space
We call sky or time;
Or during the call of the shepherd
Beyond the open field
Inside the meadows I do not see.

I did not know your name.
I tried my best to identify you.
I found you curled on the beach
Alone among the driftwood and wet stones.

I stood at a distance trying to define myself'
In the coming of this new light called rose
Or sea maid or some ordinary introduction.

You would not tell if you were of the sea
Or from some other ether or polished air.
I did not know the difference

Between the common greeting
And a moving wind against my stable self,
A wind that twirled and spun
Like a dancer expecting no applause.

You proffered your hand to me
To join you there on the sand,
One step, one step as I trusted the spirit
Of some extreme desire that we could find
Inside the amber shell.

SALVATION IS HIDDEN IN THE ROSE

***For the grace of God has appeared, bringing salvation
for all people
— Titus 2:11-14***

Salvation is hidden in the rose,
The acceptance of the texture,
The aroma, the color yellow or red,
A fullness exposed and we are less exhausted.

Farmer, astronomer, priest, maid,
The traps of a false identity,
The masks and suits and ambitions gained
Do not define the fern self, the moon self,
The depth of what it means to be a man or woman
In this century, in this time, in this little season
That holds the sun and sorrows for a moment.

The poets tell us it is the blue guitar,
Mermaids singing each to each,
When we are old and gray and full of
What keeps the context of God alive within us.

Put away your shoes and books.
Crush your diamonds into powder,
Melt the gold and gild the self
With alloys of eternity,
A formless cantata composed to
The symphony of rainwater,
The timpani of wind,
The crescendo of sea waves.

One song, one adieu from the visible world,
To the world of the single rose
Full of exaltations from the borrowed sea
Of salvation and peace.
Amen, amen I say to you
Inside the rose,
Inside the self and muted joy.

DISSERTATION

"Before we understand science, it is natural to believe that God created the universe. But now science offers a more convincing explanation."
— Stephen Hawking

I have been prepared for you all my life, Stephen Hawking,
I never understood mathematics or the use of numbers,
I have collected leaves in autumn and raspberries in July.
These have been my calculations.

You claim the existence of black holes
And an expanding universe. Bravo.
I too have claims to my black holes: the dept of the sea,
The voice of Poseidon, Africa,
The homes of Neanderthal Man, Plato's cave,
The inside of a barn in New Hampshire,
Perhaps inside the flowers of O'Keeffe.

Stars may be bits of broken matter and molecules,
But the stars I have seen
Do not translate into theory.
Unless there is a God.

Unless there is a body beyond myth,
There is no need for equations
And a race for an explanation.

There is no explanation for
Every wave between light and matter;
There is no explanation
Expect God the scientist, God the farmer,
God the voice in the chamber music.
God of the sublime silence.

You have concluded, based on science,
That all returns to dust and ere is no heaven.
You claim it is a myth for those afraid of the dark.
Have you seen the dark?

Do you know the shapes of the constellations are

Messages from God, patters and images
That translate into a prayer
Beyond the creed, Latin and old scriptures?

Yes, you are right, there are patterns to everything,
Formulas that can explain, yes, you are on the right track,
You've spent a lifetime with your chalk and computers.

I hear there is a lot to do with quantum mechanics.
Have you understood what is in the center of the fire?
Have you seen the cycles of the ivory moon?
The moon does not speak in theory;
The sun does not dance under science.

Look at the patters of the atom;
Look how everything, even under the microscope,
Turns around and around each other
Repelling and attracting.

Extend your theories to the planets circulating
Or to a man and woman embracing.
Take the measurements
And explain the mystery of the sun.
The Egyptians knew
The sun god lived inside the lioness.
Have you studied the lioness?

I have read the poets, read them all,
And I have come up with my own theories of the Universe,
My own idea about the big bang and the expansion of time.
Your books, your lectures and numbers are
Quaint figures and clever considerations. They are the myth.
They are not candles for those who fear the dark.
Why do we pretend Einstein is the gatekeeper?
Why do we worship his formulas,
Believe in dimensions that bend,
Or is it the light that bends or is eternity
Pushed out beyond the visible darkness?

Gravity begins at the center you claim,
Spinning and tossing dust and bits of matter

And we have a universe?

Yes, things spin: leaves in autumn, snow in Vermont,
Yes we now understand electrical charges,
But I too have done my research,
I too have written equations
And observed sparks from the fire,
Light from the fireflies illuminating a childhood,

Salvation is not a calculation.
Salvation does not hide inside Inflation Theory,
Or String Theory. There is more in a single kiss
Than in all your theories.
There is more in the pulse of a single man
Than in all quantum mechanics.

Take your science, take your mathematics, physics, chemistry,
theories and numbers and join us on the hillside
As we all watch a meteor shower,
Or joins us as we dance around an open fire,
Or embrace each other and sit with God, not Myth.

Listen to God, not science, Stephen Hawking.
Bundle your papers and calculations
And inhale the pure, sweet air deeply.
Close your eyes and believe in what you cannot explain.

There is no explanation except a patient God
To define the beginning and the end.

SABBATH MORNING

Ye shall keep my Sabbaths and reverence my sanctuary.
— Leviticus 19:30

The morning is a church,
The trees the naves and the birds
Confident bells
Announcing a reverence
For the rising sun.

The stained-glass ferns and daffodils
Adorn the welcome light.

There is no steeple more pronounced
Than the morning pointing upward
To clouds and sky with little worry.

The Sabbath gives the soul a place
To worship in silent prayer,
This faithful dawn our sanctuary.

SPIRITUS MUNDI

Since we live by the spirit, let us keep in step with the spirit
— Galatians 5:25

I am not a god, I am not the sea,
I am not the thunder that rattles the black sky.
Not king, not fish, not floating dust in the sunlight.

What? Words composed in the hidden corner,
Words repeated, nodding my head up and down?
Perhaps I am a madman; perhaps I am
Trapped in a cycle of crooked lines,
A bit of graphite, a smudge from the tip of a pencil.

I once thought I would be given a name,
A resume to follow. Once I thought it was my will
To act my part and play the stage for applause.

Gods drape themselves with the cloak of winter.
The sea contains the cry of the whale,
And the mystery of giant squid.
Thunder is not the drum of heaven.
A king denies the prick of a pin; fish have no magic.
A bit of dust continues on its way.

I give you one word: spirit, that space between
The match and flame, the sound before
The sound of December wind. Step out of the body,
Reject bones and blood, feel not arms and chest,
But a soft force, a suggestion we once knew,
A voice perhaps, the door opening,
The sound of the whippoorwill.

Sanity depends upon the silence of the mind.
Sanity is a straight line, paint on our fingertips
Touching the canvas as we draw a blue circle,
An iris, and we shall call the iris a god
And give the iris a purpose in the garden.
We shall name the iris sea, flame, fish, king.

GRATITUDE

Give thanks to the Lord, for he is good; his love endures forever.
— Psalms 107:1

Prayer? Have you heard
Water against the stones
During the rain?

Did you touch
The side of your face today?

When you brushed
A bit of dirt from your shoe,
Did you think about the seasons?

When you speak to an owl,
Does the owl bless you?

There are geese
Eating the distant grass.

Rains, stones, grass,
These are prayers.

Caress your face.
Our knees
Are not meant for prayer.

BEATITUDES

Earth is crammed with Heaven.
— Emily Dickinson,

Blessed are the bees
        for they make the flowers..
Blessed are the owls at night
        for they see God.
Blessed are the books
        for they store wisdom.
Blessed are the elders
        for they do not fear death.
Blessed are the children
        for they laugh in school.
Blessed are the egrets
        for they float towards the moon.

Blessed are the shadows
        for they seduce the sun.
Blessed are the men
        for they know desire.
Blessed are the women
        for they invented tenderness
Blessed are the poets
        for they touch your soul.
Blessed are they who seek heaven,
        for they will dance with angels.

PART FOUR

Gather round
Brush the dirt from your bones

A GATHERING AT THE CEMETERY

In my Father's house are many rooms.
—John 14:2-4

Gather round. Brush the dirt from your bones.
Let me hear what you have discovered in the earth.
Is the earth solid?
Did the earth carry you to a new spring?
Have you felt a different vibration in your passing?
When you inhaled your last breath
Did you inhale a new air, a liquid from the new womb?
Were you able to emerge as new pollen
Entering the next flower?

I am curious to know if what you were taught
Matches the coming rain of your new life?
I'd like to know if you can speak.
Can people hear what you are saying?
Is there a need for a kiss?
Do you need to close the widows in winter?

I am standing here reading the words etched on your stones,
And wonder if there are new words you want to say.
Do you want to rise in the night and change the words?
Instead of "Eternal Peace" you might write "There is no rest."

Here, let me make a place for you under the moonlight.
Sit beside me in the dark.
You do not have to reveal your names.
What you say will not be held against you.
We have explained to the children they will never die.
We take vows to heaven and burn incense.
We have our rituals to mock death.

What are you thinking? What have you learned
In your graves? Is there room for eternity?

A HOLY PLACE

Now the Lord God had planted a garden in the east, in Eden;
— Genesis 2:8

All I know is the light and darkness of my garden,
A place where flowers wait in the winter snow
And earth complies only in the spring heat
When I am no longer buried in a singular defeat.

No man knows the color of the rose,
Until the rose blooms among the stem and thorns,
The accent of beauty held for a moment's pause
In what has been called the exterior life.

If I bring you to the garden you will see
An ordinary fence and a few oak trees.

I share the open space with any creature
Willing to join me in this closed solitude:
The anxious squirrel, the silent butterfly,
The still rocks and soothing sky.

I make this journey at least twice a day,
Once in the morning to adjust my eyes and pray
That what unfolds hour to hour is rich and bold
In the coming of new heat and the end of the cold.

At the closing light I thank the evening stars
For guiding me to the edge of what is not too far
From what is held in the thin boundaries of this
My chapel yard.

GOD OF LIGHT

***I am the light of the world: he that followeth me shall not walk in darkness,
but shall have the light of life.***
—John 8:12

What would we see if there was no light?
Anti-matter or the opposite of existing stars?
Perhaps what emanates from sound
And the warble of a single sparrow.

Perhaps in the darkness there is a portal
To time travel, an entrance we cannot see in the light.

Perhaps inside the darkness dreams leak
Or drain into the past or into the
Future light.

There is no form in darkness so we can imagine
Shapes of things to come or things as they are.

Fossils hint at the consequence of darkness and pressure:
Ferns pressed into rocks; fish swept up from the sea
And swallowed inside the darkness of sand and stone,
Messengers of a distant shore that collapsed
Perhaps under a magnetic force,
Perhaps under the breath of God.

When light diminishes, when memory and time close in a circle,
The circle spins into a smaller circle and time and space
Do not collide; they stop like the sudden pause
Of a hummingbird at the tip of a flower,
But the bird is then, no longer a bird,
But a collection of atoms and lost energy.

Why does the earth spin on an axis?
What does this movement tell us?
Is there an encryption in the sway of wheat,
A hint in the way the tides move, a sorrow in the darkness
We cannot see, or are not allowed to see?
What if we reverse the spinning earth and the wind?

What if we turn the clock backwards
From dusk to noon to dawn again?
Until the beginning of eternity appears in the darkness.
A single spot, a single packed heat
Explained with crude mathematics.

What is the mathematical equation for happiness,
Or the theory that is condensed in the circles?
Is time in particular condensed into a single theory?
Can we prove these theories to explain the darkness
And the lack of passion? Can we prove the existence
Of invisible light and the color of the rose?

Is there an elegant equation, a song perhaps,
Notes that define the silence and the empty room?
Is there one beginning we can all believe with evidence?

Yes, the proof is in the eyes as we strain
For what we try to see in the darkness.
Yes, we dream of fire, heat, the circle that might be the eye,
Or the sun, or the hidden purpose of the elusive moon.

Something escapes the darkness, a spark, an element, a surprise,
A loose seed, perhaps a wayward pulse rejecting density.
Perhaps all is diminished into nothing from nothing born
To nothing that dies and returns always to a first impulse of light.

Combine Saturn, combine the entire universe
With a single sparrow and you have proof
There is a connection.
What is large mingles with what is small.
Power rejects weakness; heat rejects the cold.
The stars do not belong inside the breadbox.

Roll the roulette wheel
And there is chance for a win.
Roll the universe
And there is a chance
There will be ferns and flowers.
God has returned with his willow stick
Clacking along the fence that we call gravity.

Can time be reversed?
Can the tortoise run backwards
And beat the hare?

God leans back with a cup of tea and listens to the sparrow.
The existence of God is embedded inside the mind of a sparrow.
We can walk to the sea, we can sip honey, we have the ability
To create poetry and a telescope.
We invented language
And feared the locust.

Where there is life there is light.
Nothing grows without light,
But first there must be darkness
For in the darkness there is loneliness
And when any particle is alone
It seeks another and another
To merge into art or into love
Or into the aroma of coffee
In the ordinary morning
We call the sunrise.

ARGUMENT WITH THE SOUL

Yes, my soul, find rest in God; my hope comes from him.
— Psalm 62:5

I walk here through the meadow
In the early morning field,
That wide expanse of wheat and waves,
A way of looking at the sky and eternity.

The sun expands against the willing earth
And I, a single man, see my shadow stretched,
A cartoon with waving hands and arms
That mimics the dark sides
Of what it means to be a man.

If I stab my shadow, or stomp on it with my boot
It will feel no pain. An outline remains.
The body's form is not the body.
The shadow wrinkles under the virgin azure.
The morning light unfurls, a protection against
The dead light, the absence of light.

Remember at the edge of the grave?
Step back. Do not let your shadow
Weave into the open coffin.
Do not let the shadow fall into the grave
For such grave light will harm the last movement
Of the body left inside the final shadow.

This shroud is not part of the body,
Soul-like, perhaps, filigree that defines the exterior life,
A pattern of who I am,
Connected to life.

The dark imitates, the living needs protection.
I fear the rotation of the earth for time unwinds,
My shadow becomes thin and nearly disappears.
I can feel the energy stripped away from my body.
Shades of my body increase and decrease.
I have great strength in the morning.

I extend myself from this health and walk
And am equal to the strength of my shadow,
But at noon my partner is diminished,
The gray myth or soul outlined on the ground
Is invisible and I feel weak and lost.
Measure my height and girth,
Take these numbers and bury them
With the new field's foundation
Giving strength to seeds and rain
To bless the yield in autumn.

I cannot be a shadow-trader,
Offering strength pulled from the sun.
I have but one shadow.
I can count the nights in my near sleep,
Accept there are no shapes in the night,
No movement of my body that is seen,
But the shadow comes to us alone in the day,
A shifting moment moving the shape
From what we think we are: mortal,
Secure in the moment's walk.

We are not birth, not death, not sun
But nearly invisible, thin proof
There is more to life than what is seen,
Being fresh with sunlight is not false hope.

THE SKEPTIC

And behold, you shall be silent and unable to speak until the day when these things take place, because you did not believe my words, which will be fulfilled in their proper time.
— Luke 1:20

I once thought there was a solace
In the language of the flowers,
A silent swaying towards me
As I passed through the garden
Of silence in my dreaming.

What leans towards us
Is either a caress or a thorn.

I have lived enough
With the symbols of the garden:
Vines choking me when I sleep,
A serpent with an apple in its mouth,
A single rose in the afternoon
With the colors of seduction on my chest.

I made the mistake believing
There was ecstasy hidden in the garden,
A trellis with grapes
Dangling for my mouth,
The taste of the fruit,
The moisture on my tongue
To satisfy my thirst.

The trellis is empty,
The soil is no longer fertile.
Infinity of desire has turned
To the end of the day.
The incense has turned to ash.

I once believed in the lilacs,
Like the hair of a woman
Brushing against my face.
I once believed the buds of each flower

Mimicked the nipples of a woman
Offering me her nectar,
Feeding the universe with her milk,
Caressing my body with pollen.

I thought the garden
Offered unblemished fruit:
Peaches the color of skin,
Open plums the flavor
Of passion exposed,
Palm oil at the lips.

I once believed in the garden,
A primitive place where we could
Show ourselves
With unblemished nudity.

I no longer believe
There are new flowers in the soil.
Seeds will not find the earth,
Roots will not expose their stems
Or flourish in the new blossoms.

The garden is fallow.

HOPE UNDER THE AUTUMN STARS

***Be patient, then, brothers and sisters, until the Lord's coming. See how the farmer waits for the land to yield its valuable crop, patiently waiting for the autumn and spring rains. You, too, be patient and stand firm, because the Lord's coming is near.
— James 5:7-8***

At the end of summer
Children sleep
Under the constellations.
Like stars they
Rearrange themselves
In dying heat.
They no longer play
Among the asters
And late roses.
Children do not know
The name of autumn.
They feel the sudden cold
And call it alligator fur,
Or diamond clouds.
They mix what is new
With what is old.
The day's laughter
Becomes a dream
About dinosaurs
Eating pumpkins.
The best I can do
Is pretend the leaves
Are not dying.
All I can do
Is watch summer
Return to her grave
And hope for
The next resurrection
Of the lilacs in spring
And pretend
Stars will never
Be extinguished.

ARE YOU THERE GOD?

***God is our refuge and strength, a very present help in trouble.
— Psalm 46:1***

Are you there God?
I thought I heard a movement in the garden.
I know it was a deer. I know the gate
Makes a cat sound when the wind visits.
I looked for you through the darkness.
I cannot not see the flowers.

When I tap my windows I think how thin the glass
Between you and the books on my night table.

I look for you in my books. Do you write poetry?
Did you every write a novel about filling the globe
With oceans and lakes?
How did you decide what sounds to give
An egret and a whale?

At night when the sun is flirting
With the other side of the earth,
And the dew is kissing the grass,
And the dark in my room
Nearly lifts me to your company,
I touch my face and think perhaps
It is your hand on my cheek.

I am that lonely.

GENESIS

God said "Let there be light," and there was light.
— Genesis 1:3

In the beginning there was no God.
Stars succeeded on their own.
Houses rose from the imagination.
Earth was blue.

The water contained the light,
A reflection pulled from a broken sun,
A heat stored at the tips of wheat and corn
Separated from the rocks and soil,
Trees the size of an evening shadow
Draped dusk on their shoulders.

In the beginning there were two domes,
One for the sky to hang the ornaments
Of silver light, The other dome for trout ponds,
Lava and rain, an accumulation of soil,
Layer to layer, time on time.

After the light, after the water,
The swans arrived, whales, cattle,
Bees understood honey,
There were no questions,
No books and calculations.
There were the tips of a dragonfly wing,
The curl in the hair of the buffalo,
The yelp of a fox.
The sky did not need the artist's brush
To splash azure, crimson, fire
Across the waning dusk,
Just the same a man spoke,
A woman spoke,
And they shared a meal
And took possession of language,
Claimed dominion over the seas and land,
Tamed the horse and elephant,
Gave the name of flowers:

Myrtle, rose, lilacs,
Decided the stars were pictures:
A bear, a chariot, a cooking utensil.

When the earth and heavens were finished
And the kitchen towels hung on the rack,
A stillness, a solitude, a sultry light
Defined the afternoon, a time for rest
A time to imagine
The beginning and labor passed,
A time to inhale the aroma
Of herbs and spices.

A slit in the ground opened, a river formed
And new water circled around newfound treasures:
Enchantment and folly
Woven in the robes of women
Emerging from the hillsides,
Carrying silver bowls in their hands.

Men and women entered the garden for tea
And ginger cookies served from silver boxes.
The formal afternoon
Contained the language of the day: gossip,
The price of gold,
The conditions of the next hunting season.
Women broke away from the sides of men,
Imagined ecstasy and strawberries
And the sorrows of death.

Dinner was served: the side of a lamb,
The juice of crushed grapes, the taste of
Eternity touching their lips
And so they ate and drank
And claimed the earth and heavens
As their own and said there is no God,
There is no such thing as forbidden fruit,
There is no eternity without the clock

So let's dash the clock
And kiss each other's lips

And dance and possess each other
And unzip the cotton flesh from our bodies
And we are naked, unashamed
As we swim in the concrete pool
And the moon shrugs and the stars dim.

The wind arrived, the whales arrived,
The mountains spoke,
Saturn and Venus were embarrassed,
The lions were attentive.
"We are naked and not ashamed," the women said.
"We are exposed and not ashamed the men said."

"Where are you?" the lightning asked.
"Who are you?" the gods spoke
From the raging sea.
"No man, no woman has the shape of a shell,
The skin of the elephant,
The speed of the antelope.
Who is now prepared to challenge the earth
And all its creatures?"

Dust covered the land.
We had to wear the skin of the lion,
The skin of buffalo,
We had to imitate the sheep,
Clothe ourselves to make us look like we belonged,
But we did not belong,
We no longer fit among the egrets and swallows,
Among the health of earth.

We are condemned to dust,
Cursed with the pain at childbirth.
We turn away from
The morning cloak of dew
And wear rags and build homes
Made of dried sticks and clay.

We live among the thrones and thistles
With the vague memory of the rose and lilacs
And the memory of ice-cream at our lips

And the trees in summer and the one canoe
sitting still on a summer beach,
A paradise unused.

We have been shut out from the garden,
Given a hoe, expected to till the land,
We have to earn a place on the earth
Once a gift, an inheritance,
Now closed and protected
With swords and daemons who laugh
And challenge us to return.

IF GOD HADN'T CREATED YOU

It is not good for the man to be alone.
— Genesis 2:18

If God hadn't created you,
I would have created
You in a poem.
I would have extracted
The seeds of the lily
And formed your breasts.
I would have stolen bits of the sky
And formed your eyes.

If God hadn't created you
I would have taken
The earth and stones
And bathed you into being,
Baptized you with crushed stars,
And given you a name.

If God hadn't created you
I would have
Asked to borrow his breath
And hold you tightly
Until you emerged from the
Storm and wind inhaling me.

Fortunately, God made you.
He did all the work and I,
I get to write about you,
About the ease of love
And about the way you dance.

PART FIVE

I am told the morning is a blessing

DAWN'S BLESSING

***Because of the tender mercy of our God, whereby the dawn
from on high will visit us.***
— Luke 1:78

I am told the morning is a blessing,
Hidden behind the receding night
Behind the tombs of night and their shadows
Giving way to the promenade of an easy sun.

There is a reverence to the approaching light,
The shroud lifted from the pine trees, penitents
Asking forgiveness for their play at night
Having forgotten the warmth and rich soil.

I am told the morning is anointed with dew,
The air like the hands of God
Waving over each stone, each bits of grass and
The entire universe of the morning landscape.

What is holy is ordinary: the stain of wet bark,
The pale wash of blue in the indifferent sky,
The single bird preening its feathers, unnoticed.

The morning is a sheer gown, a translucent veil,
The sacred mist that falls to the ground
And dissolves the fantasy and desire of the night
And reveals the genius of the common day
Smart in its humility as we pray for mercy
Or pray for the touch of the consecrated sunlight
On our foreheads.

IT IS A PRIVILEGE TO PRAY

***Do not be anxious about anything, but in everything, by prayer
and petition, with thanksgiving, present your request to God.***
— Philippians 4:6,7

The landscape I see each day,
The expansive fields
And hidden trees,
They all ravish me with their
Space and place for me.

I have my maps and deeds
To stake my clear boundaries,
But God has given me
A way to claim
The property at his side
As he strips away
The gates and stops;
As I make my way to find
His place so large
For room and board.

Where we in heaven's place
Will stay.

I am so privileged
To linger inside God's word.
What a privilege it is to pray.

LORD HAVE MERCY

But You, O Lord, are a God full of compassion, and gracious longsuffering and abundance in mercy and truth.
— Psalm 86:15.

What have we done with the sand?
What have we done with the water?
What have we done with each other?

Heaven is not among us. Time is bleeding,
Sorrow is hidden inside each window.
We have lost the peace we kept for our neighbors.

We have forgotten our names.
Let us stir the coals in the fire,
Trace the movement of the sun,
Point the way to dawn.
There are messages in the constellations.
Do not close the door. We are not built for dying.
Where are the children?
What have we done with silence?
Are we alone? Do we fear stones?
What have we become?

One voice is many. Many voices become one.
Perhaps we have to begin again.
Perhaps we have to find the first word again.
What is prayer? What is love?
What is the dust on the African veldt?
Where did we begin?
How have we lost the path to the festival?

Gather round Let us touch each other's foreheads
In a blessing, ask for forgiveness,
Mimic the trees in autumn, shedding sorrow.
How do we find our way
Back to Bethlehem?

THE SECRET OF THE SEA

***God called the dry land Earth, and the waters
that were gathered together he called Seas.
And God saw that it was good.***
— Genesis 1-10

We asked the ocean to speak to us.
All we heard were dolphins and the scroll of the tides,
Writing in near silence rolling on the beach.
We did not ask for a spell to be cast on our bodies,
Just a song, perhaps, or an answer to the sunrise.

We are told there are secrets in the sea
So why not share them, teach us how to make coral
Tell us how to make pearls with our tongues.

Does saltwater cure our wounds?
Is the ocean an altar to float our bodies
As a sacrifice to any storm or giant squid?

We are made of salt and water.
If we listen to our hearts we may hear
Seabirds and whales speaking.

At night we fold the distant sea
Over our bodies and heave upon the waves
Until we sleep and are satisfied.

Each day God, alone at sea,
Waves his hand in the water casually
Waiting for our arrival.
We are children of the earth
Not born of the sea
Though science tells us differently.

We did not crawl onto the sand on our bellies,
And stretch our fins into legs.
We are more human than science.
We cannot collect all the shells.
One is enough, a souvenir, a gift from the sea.

As we enter the sea
we feel the currents against our bodies.
We are warned about the undertow.
We like the grip of water on our chests.
We choose not to live in the shallows,
But drown in the mouth of the sea.

Let the water, like a panther, paw our breasts,
The fur of moisture to our lips,
The claws of coral at our sides.
We'd rather be ravished by the sea
Than to run hands through
The dry sand on the beach.

We swim into the veins of the ocean,
And work our gills in the darkness.
We have tried to make a bargain with the ocean,
Offering lilies and peaches for safe passage.
But the ocean is an ogre
Seeking tribute from our tongues,
Words of beauty to describe her
And to celebrate her vanity.

We are no sea fishermen.
We can only net words.

But words do not speak to us
They murmur and roll back
Into the secret of the sea.

GOD FIRST

In the beginning God created the heavens and the earth.
— Genesis

To question where and who
Perhaps we need to take a backward glance,
Sew up the April blossoms, return them to the winter cold,
Investigate the stillness in the frozen air,
And push back to autumn's fragile death
To find the first breath that moves
The spindled earth forward.

They say all things communicate in waves,
The spirit of an elm mixed
With the air's movement for example,
Or the silence between lovers, or the wisteria
That clings to the trellis and the purple flowers shiver.

Gravity is invisible, yet it pulls and pushes.
Light bends, the universe accelerates
And we can measure hurried stars
And the explosion we do not see.

This energy we call phantom, something beyond
Our bodies when compressed and stretched,
Has the ability to penetrate all things.
A perpetual journey even in the yard picking daffodils.

We are told it is too small to measure
This space between stop and start.
If we can see the beginning we can predict the end.
I do not want to know how it is assembled.

I do not wish to look at the universe in a new way.
I prefer the flower's stability and aroma.
I am not curious to know beyond the petals and stem.

I already felt the earth and bulb in my hand
When I planted the flower last spring.

NOEL! NOEL! NOEL!

You will find a baby wrapped in cloths and lying in a manger.
— Luke 2:10-12

But Scrooge, the winter, don't you see the snow
Out the window there, beyond the darkness?
There ... the voices of children.
Don't you hear them sing Noel?
And there over the hills a family
Beside the fire making paper crowns for the morning.

There is a star, you cannot deny the star,
Not a reflection from the moon
Or a distant farmer's lantern.
Scrooge, man, witness the coming of the snow
And in the distance shepherds,
And a voice in the night, a plaintive cry.
Perhaps a lamb or a bit of wind lost in the turbulence.

But no need to speculate, for sure a child
If not the child at least what is inside you
A sudden recognition there is a sound
That is beyond our understanding but still,
A commotion in the snow past the fields and sea,
Up toward the north sky echoing the night
In a fading whisper ... Noel. Noel. Noel.
And then the silence of the lambs invades.
.

NOT MOON, NOT EARTH, BUT HEAVEN

***People will come from east and west and north and south,
and will take their places at the feast in the kingdom of God.
— Luke 13-29***

I am tired trying to climb to heaven,
Feeling the earth spin under my body,
Seeking a companion to define the rose,
Or to sway as the center sways
Since the birth of my desires.

Intimacy is a partnership.
That is why the moon does not seduce the earth,
Just caresses the cheeks of the continents
In her cycle of duty, not love.

So I sit on the veranda in spring
And reject eternity is hidden in the rose
And listen for the rumors
The moon was torn from the ribs of the earth
As I dream more of heaven.

ON WHAT CONDITION IMMORTALITY?

***Very truly I tell you, whoever hears my word and believes him
who sent me has eternal life and will not be judged but
has crossed over from death to life.***
—John 5:24

Do you wish to become forever,
A permanent memory
With a voice that echoes between the moon
And our solid dreams?

Do you wish to be like a relative
Who lives in Bombay forever
Traveling among the elephants?

Defy wisdom. Do not pay attention
To the dust at the base of the pyramids at Giza.

We are not made of just blood and bone.
Do not be fooled by the brave tombstones.
You have more genius in you.

Play with immortality, tug at it like a kite
Knowing it is not the string or paper
Draped on two crossed sticks, but the invisible wind,
A constant blush of the void blowing against our skin.

What blessing do you seek?
A guarantee the bread you bake
Will not go stale, a vigilance against the coming night?

We do not die immediately but sigh, water the zinnias,
Read a book, and then we fall into a mortal collapse,
A slow grandeur, our aura exposed
Not to heat or to frozen air but carried to
A new born sea of wounds repaired, youth restored
Deep inside the unknown bliss of our immortality.

REQUIEM

Jesus said to her, "I am the resurrection and the life. The one who believes in me will live, even though they die; and whoever lives by believing in me will never die."
— John 11-25-26

I am going to infuse into you a god,
Or a belief in a god, any god that
Brings you to blue waters of a Canadian river
Where little gods swim in the summer,
Where a single sail juts upward like hands in prayer
Or the single wing of a fallen angel.

If you do not believe in a universal God
You are forgiven; we are allowed doubt.
We remember the taste of cookie dough
On the skeleton of the eggbeater.
We remember the sound of the typewriter
Spelling words, gathering time, preparing words
To pass under a yellow Japanese arch in the garden.

We remember the purple wisteria
Spilling over our heads in summer.
These are the ornaments of those gods
Calling out our names as we ran among the ferns,
Conquered the neighbor's snow hill with our sleds,
As we inhaled the aroma of phlox
And used the dried stalks of day lilies
To challenge Sir Lancelot.

God does not wear a gilded crown
Or silken robes. God does not
Burn incense, collect money,
Twang a dirge on a guitar or piano.
Look for the god of Dunkirk.
Look for the little gods crossing
On the Queen Elizabeth,
Gathering daffodils and bleeding hearts
In the garden.
Gods of myth and legends disappear

Once the book is closed and the pages
Are pressed flat and forgotten,
But true gods rise each moment
Unexpectedly in the air that fills our lungs,
Approaches us as the autumn leaves approach us
In color, dancing around us
Like children on holiday.

True gods wash the eyes of the blind,
Build stone garden pools,
Fly paper airplanes, bake peach pies,
Play Missa Luba on the phonograph.

I write poetry, pray, sit on the porch
And feed the chipmunks by hand.
I take the power within me
That are these words
And I read them here this morning.

Do you hear an echo?
Do you remember the company at the door?
Do you remember the aroma of soup?
Do you remember the bookshelves?
The stories about Pamela the dog
And the artist on the beach of France?

There are no gods in Rome or clouds
Or in the DNA of your body.

We paint stain glass windows,
Write liturgical music, erect steeples.

Smoke curls up the chimney,
The pine trees ooze sap,

The waterfall in the garden stream
Sings at night in the August heat
Up to the open windows of our rooms.
These are the propos where little gods live.
Remember the apple tree and the half well.
Remember the salamanders and the rose trellis.

Remember the voice that first said your name.

This is not the closing of a story.
This is not the end but a present time,
A rebirth, the infusion of a spirit
Into each of us.
The beginning of a new life among us,

Little gods among us, guiding us,
Protecting us as they once did,
Now and for all eternity.

PART SIX

I know the sounds in the cemetery

WORDS OF AN ATHEIST

But test everything; hold fast to what is good.
—1 Thessalonians 5:21

I know the sounds in the cemetery:
A pleading of sorts for more air.
A request for a break in the earth.
A place more for light than roots.

The baker's son asks for warm bread.
The girl with dried flowers
Wants to breathe on the brown petals.

There, under the slab of stone,
I hear a slight tapping,
A chisel and hammer still writing poems.

If you listen closely, between the tombs,
There is a whisper, passing along secrets
From one to the other, "They have it all wrong.
We are but under-tenants of the earth."

WHAT THE SHEPHERDS KNOW

And there were shepherds living out in the fields nearby, keeping watch over their flocks at night. An angel of the Lord appeared to them, and the glory of the Lord shone around them, and they were terrified. But the angel said to them, "Do not be afraid. I bring you good news of great joy that will be for all the people. Today in the town of David a Savior has been born to you; he is Christ the Lord."
— Luke 2:8-11

Let us walk among the Lord's shepherds
And learn from the power of their staffs,
Not field, not sun, no place on earth
But in the shadow of the God's sun.

Let us walk beyond the shadows
Of the elms and oaks
That fan blossoms and leaves against the sky.
The sky does not write, does not sing
But leaves a blue wash above us
To bathe us in the light, so we may see
Where shepherds have walked,
To help us feel what others have felt
On the hillside alone listening
To the bleat of goats or the
Distant cry of a single lark.

God is not a throne or might or project.
God is the father, my father, the ferns in the yard,
The aroma of daffodils; God is the woman
Walking her dog, the sound of the carpenter
Next door on the roof of the new house.

We live in the moment between the dust
That stirs and the dust that settles.
We stretch our arms in the morning,
Believe there is time for the day's coffee
And perhaps a book and the time to
Arrange our lives in order once again.
Order breeds from chaos tamed.
I know no kings, have not sat with Cleopatra.

I ran my hand over the hieroglyphs on Egyptian *tombs
And did not feel the skin of the pharaoh.
We make false gods from how we interpret words.
We make God a convenient excuse for our own power.

God is no minstrel, no baggage to be opened
When we run out of socks.
Go to any field that is empty except for the sedge and sky,
Stand where shepherds stood, toss a stone before you,
Watch it roll and disappear; raise your hands in the air.
Feel the sun, feel the time you've had in your pockets.

Look beyond the moment and know beneath you
The earth is round, the universe long.

We are but bits of sand on the palm of God.
Follow the shepherds on the way to Bethlehem.

A BOY NAMED THOMAS

Help me overcome my unbelief.
—Mark 9:21-24

As boy I believed stones could talk,
And leaves gossiped,

And swans flew to heaven
With buckets of milk on their wings.

As a boy I believed there were
Polar bears in my socks,
And that books jiggle on my shelf.

It is easy for a boy to believe
A bicycle is made of apples and sundials,
And ice is made of cheese.

But when the boy becomes a man,
And green is green.
And pencils have erasers,

That is when he questions
"Is there a heaven?"

BE ATTENTIVE

For as woman came from man, so also man is born of woman.
But everything comes from God.
—1 Corinthians 11:12

A woman is not the rib of a man,
Not the moisture from his lips.

A woman cannot claim
She first stepped out of a man's skin,
Or felt his magic hand on her body and she
Became breasts and blood.

It is true a man is born of a woman,
But that is biology, a seed in the soil,
A rising shell from the turbulence of the sea.
Beyond biology, beyond the argument,
That we rose from the sea,

We are a combination of molecules
And bits of flesh.

Yes, it is true we have stumbled out of
The distant sun and the way the globe spins.
We have evidence we lived in caves
And kept warm under the skin of bison.
There are paintings on the cave walls
Of spears and hunters.

No matter how far back we look.
No matter what Einstein of Hawkins said.
No matter if you think your voice is made of sand,
Be attentive.

If you felt the humidity on your chest,
Be attentive.

If you wake beyond midnight and hear the owl,
Be attentive.
If you notice water is swollen,

Your skin contracting,
The wet pavement inviting you to dance,
Be attentive.

We do not have to endure God,
Just be attentive.

WHAT IS SACRED?

**Reclaiming the sacred in our lives
naturally brings us close once more
to the wellsprings of poetry.
—Robert Bly**

What is sacred, the moon?
Does the moon offer prayers?

Perhaps the sea is sacred.
We cannot drink the sea.
The salt will kill us.

What if we baptize the egrets
And make them idols?
Maybe we can return to the sun,
And build statues again to the sun,
And wear disks of gold on our chests.

Let's write psalms and sing about
The edge of ferns and how
They point towards heaven
In the humidity.

Where is the holy place?
Hidden with the drawings of bison
In sacred caves?
Food could be sacred:
Milk, peaches, the holy corn and wine.

Perhaps the voice of a woman is sacred.

I have touched the lips of poetry.
God paints the flowers.
Flowers are sacred.

THE SUN IS NOT A COINCIDENCE

I never spoke with God,
Nor visited in heaven.
Yet certain am I of the spot
As if the checks were given.
— Emily Dickinson

I read that God is dead.
I hear the children breathing.
I saw a fox last night
Illuminated under the harvest moon.
Night is a good time
To open the widow
And inhale the evening air.

The walls in my room do not whisper.
Listen to the cicadas.

My mother died. My father died.
The trees shed their leaves.
The bear curls to sleep in winter;
Snow pretends it is permanent.

We try to stop time with our photographs.

God is not dead.
The mountains bulge upward for a reason.

Touch your lips
When you are alone.
Run your thumb along your spine.
The sun is not a coincidence.

I THINK THIS IS WHAT GOD MEANS

Do not suppose that I have come to bring peace to the earth.
I did not come to bring peace, but a sword.
— Matthew 10:34

Do you think my robe is free from stains of blood?
Do you think I come this way to bring you water for your thirst?
Perhaps you believe I will chase away the tax collector,
Restrain floods, or even reduce the heat in a summer's day.
I am not a pauper with hidden gold in my pocket.

You can expect the earth will shift and break apart.
There are waves that swallow ships whole.
You may think the stars are permanent guides,
And your hunger will always be satisfied.
I have not come to bring you chocolate or peace.

I come to bring you a sword, instructions how to build a moat.
I bring you war plans and suits made of armor.

Evil has no blood. Evil does not constrict your throat when dry.
The tax collector does not have your sins on his ledger.
Evil will not flood your home, or snatch money from your wallet.
Evil is not the earth shaking, or waves chewing the hulls of ships.
Evil is a different sort of air. Evil resides in the ether of chaos.

I give you the sword made of steel compassion.
I give you the weapon of the kiss.

Evil is not inside a human form, not in shapes of what you see.

Evil Is invisible. I am your sword if you will have me.
I can be your eyes.
I can protect you if you choose, and slay evil.
Never sheathe me.

GOD OF SUNLIGHT

For the lord God is a sun and shield.
—Psalm 84-11

It is the sun, ah the sun, something Egyptian cut in stone
For the purpose to compose a first life, or death.
A place for dust, the return to dust
And definitions defined with the tip of a chisel.

See how the light was established into the stone,
Tendrils from sun to earth, from the hand to the breast,
From intentions to a spiritual notion or poetry and rest?

What center? What moisture? Seawater? Milk?
Let the surprise of nourishment wash against the open fields.
Not dew, something quick, rain perhaps, abstractions,
Foreign oils from a glass bottle.

We are held as we walk promenades, held under sunlight
Against sea whispers, cloaked in this light of lost memories.
At least there is the hint of forgiveness, a remembered voice
With no intentions to be a part of blood and poetry.

It was the sun I thought, but then a human form in yellow light,
Nothing foreign, a common suggestion: youth, silence,
The name of a rose or some small flower for my lapel
Bold in my new vest and polished shoes.

I was no huntsman, not prepared for the doe or owl or
The myth of God. We are pagan born and brought to flutes,
Icons, the skein of geese pulling spring behind them,
A mist of sorts that forms the shape of a woman,
The new April, a goddess born in the mind, prearranged.

Blue is the color of water; white the bits of seawater in a spray.
Do not provoke the contrast between the sand and the sea.
Do not claim knowledge of order and violence.
There is a single matter in the substance of the sun.

She walks along the seacoast town in a yellow gown

With choral in her hair and madness in her heart as she burns
In a single flame, bronze, gold perhaps to the music
Of the seaside café.

I am the man with a straw hat in the chair by the sea
On my veranda with a book in my hand.
The sun will disappear to my left. A shift in light
Will diminish the form; she will look in my direction.

I wave to the last line of the sun.

The beach stones are no longer white.
The surrender to the last hour is born.

PART SEVEN

In heaven's left side, the green and moss

THIS SIDE OF PARADISE

And he said to him, "Truly, I say to you,
today you will be with me in paradise."
—Luke 23-43

In heaven's left side, the green and moss,
A place to sit and consider the loss
Of what it means to be human.
There was a voice held in the body and the body
Lived among the air and earth, protected with
A layer of flesh and bone,
Something inside the fixed reason.

It is not explained at birth, this sudden loneliness,
This sudden coming of the night,
This sudden ease to breathe less of life and sense more
The liquid notion of self, a fluid movement,
Perhaps a dream or lake or restless place
Where silence is the purpose.

Paradise is divided in half:
One side for the image of self and the other
A place to collect shells
And define the shells as sea gifts.

We like sea gifts and shells. We like the taste of melon.
We like the garden ferns and the juncos at the bird feeder.

Do not tell me I am old.
Do not say I can no longer speak
Of waterfalls and anemones as though they no longer exist.

I understood the language, once, of the woman
Who made silver bracelets.
They say she no longer lives by the sea.

Every woman lives, once, by the sea. It is their obligation,
The urgency to return to the salt water,
That place where right and left have no meaning,
Where they immerse themselves in the water

And they become less women
and more visible to the sea foam.

Perhaps it is the sea foam curling
At the edge of sleep on this,
the right side of paradise.

HYMN

Sing to God, sing praises to his name; lift up a song to him
who rides through the desert; his name is the Lord; exult before him!
— Psalm 68:4

Listen to the winter chants,
Holy words, the coming of God
Or the sound of a God
Squeezed out of the frozen ground
Where stone and earth combine
Into a solid platform.

Let each note blend with the next
In the cadence of morning bells
Or the murmur of children
Born and more waiting to be born
Inside the sea-place.

Cold is the day,
Harsh the voice of men,
Misdirected, if soul and desire
Are marked for satisfaction
And not for the union of purpose.

Holy prayers open to the song,
Open to the revelation of self
In the body's fragrance,
In the taste of self and the other;
And, then the hymn resounds.

DEEP INSIDE THE WINTER LAKE

Have I not commanded you? Be strong and courageous.
Do not be frightened, and do not be dismayed, for the Lord,
your God, is with you wherever you go.
— Joshua 1:9

Now is the time to challenge the cold,
To lift the wool coat and open the door.

The maw of winter will strike the face
With sudden force and brutal intentions.

It was my choice to visit the lake
That gave itself to ice and snow
And think that water still holds itself
In liquid form far beneath the surface
Where silence holds the little heat
That battles the final stiffness.

I wore my leather gloves, my fur cap
And boots of black rubber.
Because I walked quickly in the snow
(My breath curled in little clouds)
I beat the frost and artic air
And strayed to a foreign heat
And believed in what I believe
And did not surrender to the bitterness
That draped itself on the shoulder
Of the white hills.

MARRIAGE PROPOSAL

Do everything in love.
— 1 Corinthians 16:14

Pilgrim. Greetings in your silence.
No need to speak. I will speak.
I am the dream bard.
I gather suffering, bits of stone,
A day's sunlight and arrange it all
For you like pears in my arms.
A fruit that yields sweet liquid,
Perhaps a nectar.
Perhaps a substance that blends
With our blood and time,
Something in the cycle of a cherished life.

We pack our bags with trinkets of the past:
The last words of the grandmother,
Geese that merged with the closing of the day,
The ferns that once stood as sentinels
While children in their compliance listened
For the coming rain.

You do not speak.
Do you know the language of the dead?
Do you accept that the dead
Continue to gather their bounty,
Dream of green boats
On the surface of a summer lake,
Laugh in the presence of women bowing,
Once in greeting, once in supplication,
Once in reverence to the sorrows of forgiveness?

Will you join me here in my dreaming?
There is no love where there is no journey
Built on this first greeting.

THE NEW TESTAMENT

I rejoice at Your word as one who finds great treasure!
— Psalm 119:162

I have come to tell you there is a God.

Parades are easier to prove, the fandango
With castanets and guitars and a red dress.

Perhaps your God is not made of bone and earth.
Perhaps your God does not reside
Half year in the circus tent
The other half in a field of barley.

There is a clown God who wears a mask
And a painted smile. Hoo! Hoo!
The balloons and the giant shoes
And watch out for the squirting flowers!
But do not be fooled
With the silk fabric and crooked hats.
It is good to believe God can make us laugh,
But that is not the God I found.

I bring you the news that God is not an old man
Though he thinks like an old man:
Looking back, recognizing the names of mountains,
Breathing as he once breathed when he was young
Pursuing the antelope, buying saltwater taffy
At the shore, even lying in the sun.

That is the hint of God, the sun above
And the way we all cast a shadow in the image of God,
In the daily breath we inhale as we circulate our blood.
Place your hands on your cheeks and feel the softness.

I heard you have looked for God
In the fields in autumn.
I heard you burnt offerings
In marble temples, among candles and urns.
God does not ask for trinkets and painted windows.

He smiled when Michelangelo drew on the ceiling.
Yes, yes homage can be paid, but homage to
The trapeze artist and to the tame lions, homage to
The wheat, to the corn, homage to the pomegranate
And thunder that brings the rain, but homage to God?

God likes you to visit with your stories.
Bring your daughters, your sons and lovers.
God understands the contours of your body.
He delights in the way people touch each other.
God does not slap your knuckles with a ruler.
God does not wear silk slippers in Rome.

I saw God.
He lives in Brooklyn sometimes.

REPORT TO THE SKEPTICS

And have mercy on those who doubt.
—Jude 1:22

I have gone to my books in search of certitude,
Turned page to page, read sentences and words,
Imagined what the writer imagined;
And, still, I cannot find proof that stone is stone
Or my voice is the voice of self.

We believe the echo is evidence of existence,
We believe the heart circulates blood
Inside the body, but I do not believe in blood
Or the heart but more in the other system,
The place for lilacs and the sound of Russian chants
In the cathedrals capped in spiral seashells.

Doubt opens the earth and collects what is left:
The discarded body, the slow disintegration
Of shape and bone similar to the last snow receding.

Doubt disturbs the patterns: why not spring proceeding autumn,
Or death first and then suckle at the mother's breast?

I have not concluded my investigation,
The hunt for rose thorns
That prick the soul's existence
Continues.

A BLESSING

Comfort ye, comfort ye my people, saith your God.
— Isaiah 40:1

Be of comfort for God is in your garden,
Inside a fern, perhaps, or the autumn rose.
Receive the aroma, the whispered scent
That there is hope, in the fallen seeds,
For the next spring.

Leave behind the desert of self and make way
For the wilderness to expand
Into what you think is your wasteland.

Each valley in your waking,
Every crag on any mountain scar,
All will be made bright and easy
In the coming of the day.

Trust the phantom air,
A coming light that lingers:
A recognition. Your mother's voice
Or the voice of your grandfather,
Some ancient traveler agreeing
He is still there beside you.

Yes, grass dies in autumn and flowers fade,
But God will not abandon you.
He will return with His buckets of paint
With His brushes and reinstate beauty
One stroke at a time as you watch
And see with your new eyes.

The word will haunt you in the beginning,
Vague, not exact, a murmur even,
But there will be a sound you recognize:
The heartbeats in the womb,
Cries in the cities, the silence in any meadow,
The same voice, the same encouragement.
There will be arms extended to embrace you.

At first you will think they are the arms of a lover;
But more than love, more than flesh and satisfaction,
There is the embrace of your hidden self,
The soul-self, the self that carved pumpkins,
Swam in rivers and held a caterpillar in your hand.

You will be fed from the hands of God.
Taste fresh bread and take counsel,
Take morsels of wisdom, and you will be blessed.

Be not all nations but a single island
Draped with a necklace of coral around your neck.
Accept your place in the ocean
That caresses all the edges of you.

All vanity, all arguments are put aside in your solitude.
How do you compare to God and to the God's wishes?
Do you possess magical potions that make seeds into flowers?

Have you been reading the constellations?
Remember God sits on the earth, instructs dolphins,
And choreographs their movements in the water?

Do you remember the distance between heaven and earth?
Do not plant without conviction.
Do not sow the fields without the promise
Of summer's heat.

Look around.
The blade of grass did not create itself.
God is not fickle like the seasons.

We are given strength in the generosity of God
Who offers hope and compassion,
Who touches our foreheads with a blessing.

THE SECRETS

Would not God discover this? For he knows the secrets of the heart.
— Psalm 44:21

It is the secret inside the ferns and distant light we seek,
Inside the sun, perhaps, or spinning tightly inside the trees.

Born for a moment's glimpse of
Seeds and seasons,
Honeycombs and ragweed,
We live inside false wisdom and common exteriors.

Let us whisper upward towards the light.
Let us admit there is more inside the fusion of the sun
Than inside all our sighs at night when we believe
We understand the night air that surrounds our bodies.

Right is the color of the autumn trees: mottled,
Varied, filled with the promise of the next season.
Right is the sea wave like a woman breathing.

We are the interlopers dividing each day
As though we own eternity.
Braggarts with our books and voices
We pretend we understand the innocence of the landscape.

The buds inside spring allow us to trespass
In anticipation of their beauty.

Let us admit what we know; God is tender.
Death divides the seen from the unseen.
Time extinguishes the hour.

COMPLINE

***Then Jesus told them, "You are going to have the light just a little while longer. Walk while you have the light, before darkness overtakes you."
— John 12:35***

Some prefer the light of morning,
The hay light, light on our hands
Like peach light, the coming of the day.
Like a veil drawn from a gypsy's face.
Bells and painted wagon wheels.
The arrival, kettles rattle,
And the harness of each horse stretched.
Such good leather and the burden born
Again to break the silence.

I'd rather drink the honey light of day's end,
Amber, a yellow lacquer on the trees,
A final sweep of Rembrandt's brush.
Women at the lush fire and the children,
Little flames of light illuminate
The silver buttons and clothes they wear.

The sun descends inside the night,
Little, little, less the yellow light,
The blush of innocence and acceptance.

There is no better light than this
To give the children a single thought to sing
        AMEN:
To the sun dying in these hands of ours,
    To the bronze self,
     To the ochre self,
To the closing of the last day's hour.

THE FARMER'S APOLOGY TO GOD

Remember this: Whoever sows sparingly will also reap sparingly, and whoever sows generously will also reap generously.
— 2 Corinthians 9:6

Perhaps I can explain in a poem
The condition of your existence in my field of stones.
I spent many years clearing the land
In preparation of each new harvest.
At winter's end, in the first breaking of the soil,
I asked myself the purpose to plow and sow.

In part it was to fill the space between meeting you
And the parting when I left you there beside the sea
And I knew you were not willing
To dream your dreams with me.

How do I build a daily purpose with my horse and hoe
When long ago I found the cure
And what I know to be the illness
Behind my slow breathing?

The earth has been my writing board;
The wheat and barley my poems that fill the barn
As farm and land and seasons wend their way
Each day to day from time begun
To time that ends.

When was my life ever as easy as during the days
Of your voice and teasing?
I wish I had claimed you for my keeping
For now it is my need to satisfy
The hymn of loss and blooms that magnify
The seasons closed and renewed.

How much easier it would have been in my harvest
To turn my field and stones and find
The company of you in my daily choosing.

Each night I brush the dirt from the plow

And hook the reins on the barnyard door,
Artifacts that seem harsh and rude.

And not the fruits and seeds
That could have been you

PART EIGHT

I've been to some distance beyond the curl of the sea.

THE HOLY MAN SPEAKS TO HIS WIFE WHO HAS JUST DIED

The Lord is near the brokenhearted and saves the crushed in spirit.
— Psalm 34:18

I've been to some distance
Beyond the curl of the sea,
Beyond the tallest pyramids,
Past sacred cows and rice fields.

I know it was a foreign land, humid,
A place where there were rumors
Of tigers and airplanes
Landing once a month to deliver supplies.

I could unfold my old maps and point with my finger
There, to the north of this peninsula,
And here, between this river and mountain,
A passage to the father-place, the ancient grove
And a distant clatter of hooves, cranes painted
On the splash-blue sky.

It was there where I learned of you,
Perhaps not your name, but an ancient silver bell
To be worn on the forehead,

I have seen children
Pretend they are elephants
Bathing In the river, lifting their arms
From their sides like trunks.
Little girl elephants
Rocking back and forth on their knees;
Little boy elephants
Stomping in the mud.
I have worn down my worry beads
Into smooth flat stones,
Burnt sticks of bamboo to your memory.
I remember how you dyed your hands
In the ceremony of fidelity.

Watch how I sprinkle the earth with palm oil.

I dip my fingers into the marriage bowl.
It is the custom to say your name three times
As the oil is released from my hands
Like coins tossed into the streets
At the time of the spring festival.

You stay with me
In the smoke of the bamboo.

**UNCONTROLLABLE LAUGHTER AROSE
AMONG THE BLESSED GODS**
— Homer c. 700 B.C.

He who sits in the heavens laughs.
— Psalm 2-4

Why does God laugh
Sitting in a circle eating pomegranates,
Listening to the sea roll back and forth
Across the earth?

Does God hear what I do not hear?
Vespers? Water dripping from the melting ice?
The robin celebrating the afternoon sun?

Is God in consultation with the swans,
Referring to maps,
Pointing to the outer ridges of the universe,
Or at least to the edge of my yard?

Does God hear the gossip of lions,
Question the silence of the goldfish
Swimming slowly under the ice?

What does God know that I don't know:
The valley is female, and water is male.

What is God's humor and authority: Wisdom?

Does he have bearskins wrapped around his shoulders
To keep warm?

We are born to achieve greatness, to build and conquer!
We have come by way of the fire from the hilltop!
We rule the whales and the albatross,
And yet I still hear
God's uncontrollable laughter.

GOD OF THE FOREST

The Lord is near to all who call on him, to all who call on him in truth.
— Psalm 145:18-19

I've been out this evening talking to the trees,
So you would think I was crazy
If you were hidden in the tall grass
And heard my conversation as I looked upward.

I know the sound of the forest god
When he passes above the trees,
As his robe brushes against the leaves.
Some people think it is the wind.

I pretend that I see God. He looks like my grandfather
In beige pants carrying a cup of coffee to the veranda.
So I speak to him in the way I speak to the geese
As they fly overhead. I discuss the journey, perhaps
The temperature, surly my desire to join him at his travels.
Sometimes he stops and looks down, extends his arms
And says the ocean was particularly blue that day,
Or the earth continues to spin accurately, and I am assured.

I sometimes tell him I no longer believe in heaven
And he rains down heaven upon my head and I am covered
In petals, or thunder depending on his desire to comfort me.

So I step into the woods two, sometimes three times a week,
And call out his name, and he appears. Sometimes we speak.
Sometimes I wave my hand above my head
And sometimes he waves back at me.

EVE

The man called his wife's name Eve,
because she was the mother of all living.
— Genesis 3:20

I

All beginnings contain water, or the feel of water,
A condense universe of distant time when
Matter and idea formed into the shape of what is to come.
It is said love suggests water.
I stand at the side of the mountain stream,
A lasting source of silver ideas, a calming sound,
And define the fold of your voice in this borrowed time.

II

What is it the whale discovered in the blue middle
Of a world given to the whale that we do not know?
We are all contained in the voluminous matter,
Pushed back and forth between the center and the edge.
We recognize a brushing against our skin as we push forward,
As though we were formed from clay or a divine truth.
Let us be embraced by the ocean's robe, the first source,
The beginning of a new washing as we die into a new life,
Live in a second death, the coming of the siren or second self:
You, transparent still, the idea of beauty formed in the gods' myth.

III

What is the purpose of the adventure, the purpose of the rose
That sits in the distant garden under a shadow?
What is beyond the invention of the first sighting?
Clever are we who believe we have seen the making of love,
The stirring in the garden that made a rose, or the boiling
Water at the sea foam condensed in a single refrain,
Convinced we have found the single argument made
To defend the choices to flourish against the splendor
We define as splendor. Take not what the scholars sell.
It is the self that is instructed in desire and poetry.

Throw away the maps and compass. She that comes
Does not recognize numbers and proof there is a north or south.
She that slumbers at the shore, she that sings your name
Is the north and south; she is the sea wail and blue hymns.

IV

It all begins in the water, the coming of spring.
We share the first impulse to rake the soil and dream of zinnias.
We do not die in winter but maintain the call to satisfy
What we choose. We are not unconscious bears.
We do not abandon the candor of our bodies.
We begin with the caress, the first rain perhaps.
We once believed the astronomers knew the answers:
The cosmic wave created bits of matter then joined
To form a mass of light and energy that is contained
By the pressure to hold together.
There is more to be found in the palm of a lover
Than in all the stars that congeal in the open universe.
That is why we believe in the single flower.

V

Eve was not our idea. Some say the serpent drew his skin
Around her elusive shape to form the lines of her body.
Children color inside the lines. We build fences and deeds
To define what belongs to us in our labor and assumed trust.
We forget we belong to a different earth, a distant place
For whispers and thunder combined, a prayer perhaps
In the coming of the day, the recitation of a poem,
Or the notion of your name. We do not know how we arrive
At the conditions of the mind, what sticks to form the house,
What measure to weigh what it is we seek,
But we recognize the formation of the clouds
And the sudden scent of the sea when we slowly arrive at the sea
And so we fill in the empty spaces with the cycle of ourselves,
Childhood first and so then to our old age all a single truth:
We lean back into the fruit of the living one, born out of dust,
Given over to her benediction under the wave of her hand.

VI

The astrologists made their attempt to etch into the night's sky
Pictures of bears, lions, giant crabs, the goat and fish.
We fear the claws and the distant roar of savage nights.
There are stories of giant squid tearing down sea trawlers,
Stories that little boys turn into goats with horns and
Cloven feet. We have heard about witches and how they
Cover their bodies with silk and paint their faces
With damp rose petals and crushed pearls,

But she that steps out of the sea arrives on the shell,
She that wears the necklace of pearls, strokes the bear,
Knows the name of every lion. Do not trust the star painters.
They do not caress the light with their hands.

VII

To be in the world and not know water on our lips,
To stand at the end of what is dry and never swim in love,
Sends us to an empty valley, no proof of a fluid life,
No trace of ancient ferns or fossils of limber fish.
The stalk of self withers under a callous sun.
Clods of parched earth will not produce a harvest.
From ancient dust to ancient purpose we return
To a changed season as we hope to relinquish a former self
And give ourselves over to the new air that will take us
To a visible thought, a vague outline of what is to come,
A shadow, perhaps a vision, something holy or mythic.
It does not matter which. We believe in the seeing.
It is in the transparent snow and painted rain.

VIII

The wings of the hawk spread out and return together.
This is flight inside the disturbance of the air,
A movement combined with muscles and bone.
There is no greater explanation than this.
What is joined lets loose upon the world a new notion:
A summer lake is formed inside the cup of a worn land;
Wind that seeks the trees is no longer wind
But a hollow rush and stream through the neighborhood.
Certitude is not a mustard seed in the closed hand

But a sowing, an explosion of pollen, kernels breaking,
The earth opening her door again and again.
Conviction is not an imagined thing but hay in the barn,
Apples, straw in our hair, melons and sweet juice.
When a woman brushes the sand form her feet,
When she exhibits two open palms,
When she has dough under her fingernails,
Recognize there is an invitation to join her there.

IX

Beauty may appear to be lost in an undulating sea,
Pushed back into Poseidon's fury, prone to weakness,
Thrust to the violence of the coming storms.
But if we bathe inside the blue water, lounge in routine,
If by chance we see the funnel of a frigate
And point to the distant smoke, perhaps we can speak
To the horizon, acknowledge there is no edge to the sea
But a sudden recognition that a fluid path lays bare before us.
The labor of hope is curled inside the constant waves
That lure us one step at a time into the water.

X

A man is built of stone: stiff, solid, heavy for the lifting
Arranged at the edge of a field, cleared for a smooth planting.
No man has the vision of a soothsayer, a predictor of ease,
But stone can be transformed into fine grains of sand,
A future can be arranged with the help of wind and water
Washing over us day to day, pulling us down into the stream
To become the stream, a liquid self, drawn down to the giving sea.

XI

In the end it is the water, not heat, not stars, not the bears
Or the condition of the clouds.
We once believed it was the coming of spring that defined
The order we seek. It is not the spring, not the
Hidden roots or sagging trees.
Somewhere there is an exception to what we believe,
A visage that does not define what we imagined,

But more what has imagined us to be in the face of the other.
I walk along the shore with a lantern,
Rock the light back and forth to warn distant ships
That they will soon crack against the rocks if they do not turn away.
I pretend this is the main purpose of such light.
I've heard rumors of mermaids, remembered a certain voice,
Read a poem or a line in a book about Russian winters
And ever since I have lived with a human wish:
To sway the lantern above my head to implore,
Beseech Eve to step out of the water, out from the poem,
To form a plain shape in my dreaming so reason may rest
In the uncertain promise of the next cold evening.

FAITH

The apostles said to the Lord, "Increase our faith."
—Luke 17:5

I no longer believe, if so believing requires
The memory of incense, holy words,
Stories of saints and popes in silken robes.
Truth is not divided from soul and body to explain
The difference between soul and body,
Perhaps the eternal service to the festival of ourselves.
Deny breath and blood contain certitude,
And we deny the howl, the night cry,
The intervention of sorrow in the blue light.
Strike the soul with palm branches. Ignite the fires.
Train the smoke to mimic memory, a trance, a gimmick
Of common black birds eating the seeds on the flat snow.

Faith is a fish on the dock: mouth gapping, colors fading,
And still the fish is able to squeeze life from the water
Passing through its gills, and yet still the bleeding,
And the children come to watch as the fisherman
Cut off the head of the fish and the boy says
"The eyes still see. The fish does not close its eyes."

I may be eccentric in my choosing not to conspire
With the unseen garden, not to cavort with imagined trees
Or to consider the sound of bees a whispering god.
I accept the visit of the osprey, the severity of its wings,
The talons hooked to the branch. I admire the bulging whales,
Black in their skin, sleek in their cutting into the sea waves.

I do not need proof of the physical world to acquaint myself
With bones, stillness, reveries of horses and girls.
I do not need to deny August heat, the quality of stars.
I do not need to disavow blessings, whispers, and soul logic
To believe in paradise.

Faith is an idle walk along the ocean shore
Where we know the name of the taffy vendor.

GOD LOVES YOU

First God, then love.
—Anonymous

God is a salmon upstream.
God is the dew.
God is the easy way
The egret lifts her body
From the shallow water.

God is in your tea.
Do you know
The name of God:
Wheat, Hyacinth, Hail?
Have you see God with
The shawl of a lamb?
God is your neighbor
Cutting the grass and waving.

When you place
The shell to your ear,
God is whispering
The dimensions of the sea.

God is not sitting
On the moon wearing
The rings of Saturn on his finger.

When you sleep,
God taps your forehead
As you dream there are giraffes
In your room
Nodding their approval.

GENESIS

He set the earth on its foundation, so it should never be moved.
— Psalm 104:5

They say there is a new way to the center,
Something said with light and speed,
A way to consider the beginning,
A first explosion, the disturbance of
Nothingness into chaos, a scattering of
Bits and heat, waves of magnetic poles
Confirmed in the calculations,
Evidence gathered in smears of dust.

I choose what is old: the aroma of haystacks,
The scoop of the crescent moon, August ease.

I do not wish to consider less than these
Held together in a photo album,
Arranged one by one with little words
Written in white ink:
"The Grand Canyon"
"At the seashore"
"The circus bear"

I do not wish to know with certitude
The dimensions of space and antimatter.

I will keep what is blue and flat,
What resembles the labored sea.

I remember the paws of the dancing bear
How they rose up above the bear's head
As I extended *my* two open hands
Above *my* head and roared.

AUTUMN PRAYER

Do not be anxious about anything, but in everything by prayer and supplication with thanksgiving let your requests be made known to God.
— Philippians 4:6

I'd like to bring my brush and imitate the autumn trees.
There are no other choices but these
To consider in a round shape of an October dream.

Farewell to the brilliance of August green,
Gentler once in the former place or memory.

She has grown old in dust and forgotten reveries
Against the flight of geese and lower fields.

Let's yield to the sound of a single stream.

Oh that I may turn with the orange and yellow,
Disrobe and be innocent in my walking
As we are found among the dry corn stalks
At the rendezvous once again.

I can recreate the color of dried wheat,
Mix the pigment of pumpkins and squash
Into a hushed tone of an autumn glaze.

Let the vines droop and white flowers fade.
It was enough to admire bits of fruit and heaven
If such place exists in the damp passion of this:
A forbidden hymn in some abundant bliss
So exposed in the blush of this last season.

BRUSH THE EARTH WITH YOUR OPEN HANDS

***God himself that formed the earth and made it; he hath established it,
he created it not in vain, he formed it to be inhabited.***
— Isaiah 45:18

It is time to dig into the earth, not a grave, not to plow,
Not to hunt for treasure. It is not that sort of earth
Where stones and moisture collect.

I do not even consider the time as you consider time.
You've heard there are seasons, dates on a calendar.
I speak about the fish in the blue, Sargasso Sea,
The month of corn and harvest moons,
The sort of time that is considered in your room
When there is the last amount of darkness.

We have lived a wingless existence,
Broken apart the shells of self and vigor,
Turned ourselves away from the Greek pose,
The Viking ships, the Inca gold.
There is no time left to place on the walls.

Come with me to the north field.
Let me point out the shades of green in the grass,
The way the leaves shudder in a blue wind.
You have forgotten the way of the earth,
The way of seeing what has come before you.
There was the earth before the voice in the fields
Pulling horses to open the ground.

We have turned ourselves away from the aroma of the earth,
Forgotten the perfume of spring and the blush of the rose,
All from the earth, all from the center of the living roots,
All unlocked from the stones.
It is not a dream; the colors are not fading.
The horn in the distance might be the owl,
Might be the roe buck, or the cry of the shepherd
Advancing to the next field.

The city does not know the seeds,

Does not have bits of wool on its shoulder.
What erupts from the center does not hold
Unless it is the soft pulp of the mushroom,
Unless there is the intelligent flax and easy corn.

We have lost the ether of the clouds, the moisture of rain.
We did not know we had to choose between
The condition of the iron spike and the stem of the rose.
There is a solution to our dreaming, a way to fold ourselves
Into the ferns and retain the inheritance of our daring.

Follow the crow to the forest; guess the size of the bear,
Place yourself in the possible condition of a sunrise.
We are the primitive players, rubbing mud against our chests,
Drawing lines of paint onto our faces. No longer belonging to
The centuries. We know nothing of centuries.
Let us divide our time between the cables of the sun
Pulling us up in the morning and the night amber
Nearly distinguished if it were not for the last spark of moon.

We have survived the thickets, stepped out of the imagined beast.
We no longer consider ourselves similar to the wolves.
Let me show you the difference between the tattered earth of self
And the fruit found cascading down like water from a tree.
Do not confound your vision and call the garden an opportunity.
Do not wear masks, concealing you are children of the Neanderthal.
Do not claim tradition and the false rights of man.

Remember the spine of the feather. Converse with the dew.
Dress as the azaleas dress, seduce the nightingales,
And brush the earth with your open hand.

THE NEW ASTRONOMY

God made the two great lights, the greater light to govern the day, and the lesser light to govern the night; the stars also.
— Genesis 1:16

Yes, that is it, a cut on the skin,
A taste of the orange, perhaps the bear
Scraping against the ragged earth.
No doubts, no questions,
Just certitude brought to us in
The voice of our fathers from a distant
Time, where smoke cleared from the
Glade, a battle won or lost,
A summer mist dissolving, and there
Standing, a silhouette, a recognized form
Or state or vision.

At first we thought
It was a woman that transformed herself
Into a tree, so not the tree or woman
But some form, a flat stone in our hand,
The picture of a great aunt feeding
The ducks at Luna Park.

At once
We thought it was all for death,
A neglected vision at the closing time,
The earth unfolding and folding.

We thought there was no God,
Not even the flame at vespers.

How easy to dismiss theology.
How easy to turn the pages and sleep
That night and dream there were no gods,
No horse with wings, no stars
In the shape of chariots.
We thought we were champions,
Good to outsmart the cold,
Able to plot our next meal,

Record evidence of sorrow and the cure.

There is more to man
Than clocks and hay fields,
More to death than lost appointments.

In the holy end there is a beginning.

Sorrow bleeds to joy
And so joy defines
The new astronomy.

www.ingramcontent.com/pod-product-compliance
Lightning Source LLC
Chambersburg PA
CBHW052146070526
44585CB00017B/1992